ROSWELL

Historic Homes and Landmarks

ROSWELL

Historic Homes and Landmarks

A Collection of Drawings
by
ERNEST E. DeVANE

Text by
CLARECE MARTIN

Published by
THE ROSWELL HISTORICAL SOCIETY, INC.
Roswell, Georgia

ARTIST'S NOTES

Any statement of how this book came into being must necessarily begin with a lesson in perspective I learned from the scroll of an old Chautauqua desk in the family home in south Georgia.

The curious little wall-hung desk was the equivalent of a child's encyclopedia of today. The blackboard front dropped down to become a writing table with a row of tiny pigeon-holes behind it. Mounted on a pair of hand-cranked rollers above the blackboard was a scroll on which was printed a series of lessons covering an amazing variety of subjects. My favorite lesson was one showing how to draw a Greek temple in proper architectural perspective.

Fascinated by the vistas perspective revealed to me, I drew houses and roads vanishing to points on distant horizons until stacks of sketch books rose like small mountains around the walls of my room. From this simple beginning grew a career in art and a life-long interest in the architectural heritage of my native state.

Art school in Atlanta opened other vistas to me. Already familiar with the elegance of Savannah and coastal Georgia, I was introduced to the beauty of middle and upper Georgia by a host of new friends.

Paralleling my interest in architecture was my love of portrait painting, two things separate, yet wonderfully compatible. Upon graduation I planned to travel about the south dividing my time between painting portraits and making drawings of historically significant homes and buildings.

World War II intervened, however, and when I returned to Atlanta after three years' service with the army in Europe I found things much changed. Commercial art was riding Atlanta's rocket to expansion. So I turned my talents in this direction.

Drawn like so many others to the beautiful hills north of the city, my wife and I subsequently built a home near Roswell. This close proximity increased our awareness of the urbanization threat to the fine old town.

We were therefore delighted when the tide of concern for historic preservation produced historic area zoning action by the city council, the formation of the long needed Roswell Historical Society, and the restoration of Bulloch Hall as a house museum.

It is my hope that those who look upon this book with pleasure will also feel the need to help preserve not only Roswell and some of the last remaining vestiges of our heritage in the Atlanta area, but also the heritage of our state and country as a whole. For without love of our roots and knowledge of our past we cannot build the future.

Ernest E. DeVane

FOREWORD

The historic treasures of Roswell, the ancestral homes, the ancient landmarks, the continuing abundance of nature, live on through time. Early Roswell families arrived on the North Georgia frontier in 1838 as the Indians headed westward. Within a few years the settlers had forged a thriving and cultured community out of a wilderness.

Coastal planters long had coveted the Indians' rich alluvial farmlands while watching their own sandy soil depleted by yearly cotton crops. They yearned too for the mild and healthful climate of the uplands. When gold was discovered on North Georgia Cherokee Land in 1828, treaties soon were drawn for the land, and arrangements made for the Indians' removal.

Prospectors, tradesmen, and settlers swarmed into the goldrush towns of Auraria and Dahlonega. The Bank of Darien sent a representative, sixty-four-year-old Roswell King, a man of great vision and enterprise, to establish a branch of the bank in Auraria.

He followed Indian trails to the Chattahoochee River and crossed into Cherokee land near the mouth of Vickery Creek. Here the Blue Ridge foothills begin their rise to join the great Smoky Mountains of Tennessee and North Carolina. Massive forests stretched beyond sight, and untamed mountain streams rushed to the river.

Roswell King, manager of coastal plantations for forty years, was aware of the possibilities of this verdant land. He envisioned a mill powered by the waters of Vickery Creek and a thriving village close by. He acquired vast acreage made available by government land lottery after the Indians' departure. He built a substantial log cabin with glass windows and floors of pine, and later supervised the construction of a dam and millrace on the creek. With the aid of his son, Barrington King, he was able to realize his dream of a cotton mill on the banks of Vickery Creek.

Roswell King offered homesites to old friends in Savannah, Midway, Sunbury, and Darien, strong and courageous people who would leave their comforts and possessions and found the new settlement of Roswell.

This book is a tribute to these pioneers who called themselves "the colony," to their enduring homes and landmarks, and to their descendants who have cherished and preserved these historic treasures of Roswell.

Clarece Martin
Roswell, Georgia

ACKNOWLEDGMENTS

Among the many satisfactions realized during the development of this book has been the fact that while many people were involved because of the very nature of the undertaking, the good spirit and complete cooperation of all insured accomplishment. And it is significant to note that everyone participating in producing this publication, short of printing and binding, is a member of the Roswell Historical Society. The book is indeed a publication of the Society.

Special thanks must go first to the owners of the historic homes and buildings which are the prime reason for creating the book:

Allenbrook	Mrs. Barnett A. Bell
Barrington Hall	Miss Katharine Baker Simpson
Bulloch Hall	Mr. and Mrs. Richard S. Myrick
Goulding House	Mrs. James I. Wright
Great Oaks	Mr. and Mrs. Emmett R. Rushin
Holly Hill	Mrs. Robert (Evelyn Hanna) Sommerville
Mimosa Hall	Mr. and Mrs. C. Edward Hansell
Minton House	Mrs. Dennis Lackey
The Old Bricks	Mrs. Arthur W. Smith
The Roswell Presbyterian Church	The Congregation
Primrose Cottage	Mr. and Mrs. Charles N. King
Roswell Stores	Mr. and Mrs. Richard S. Myrick

We are indebted to Miss Katharine Simpson for her valuable assistance in supplying historical data; to Mrs. Henry Wing and Mrs. R. G. Ezzard who reviewed all text material for authenticity of historical detail; to Peggy Black for her expertise and care in proof-reading text material and final galley proof; to Janet Russell for her experience and sound guidance in all details of publication; and to Marty Barnes and Jean Baird for their effective handling of promotion and distribution, ably assisted by Marie DeVane.

The original idea for publishing the book had to be approved by the Society's Board of Directors and its Executive Committee. Without this approval and the sustained support and encouragement of both bodies the project could not have been accomplished.

The Public Relations Committee of the Roswell Historical Society has been responsible for planning all aspects of the book, and for executing its publication. The Committee is composed of Mark Collis, Ernest DeVane, Clarece Martin, Heath Rushin, Janet Russell, Lucy Yankee and the editor. If this book can rightfully claim achievement of quality and a meaningful contribution to Roswell's and to Georgia's historical records, major credit must go to this Committee for its loyalty, hard work and patience with the infinite details always involved in such a publication — but most of all for its collective determination to produce a volume in which the Roswell Historical Society can take great pride.

Emmett Rushin,
Editor and Committee Chairman

CONTENTS

PLATE I

ALLENBROOK

ALLENBROOK

Atlanta Street

Built in the early 1840's as an office and residence for the manager of the Ivy Woolen Mills, this two-story house overlooked the mills and dam from a bluff high above Vickery Creek. Hand-moulded clay brick were set in an uneven course, with interesting designs at the windows and cornices, softening the simple salt-box profile. The house has solid brick walls eighteen inches thick and heart-of-pine flooring twelve inches wide. Brick fireplaces in each of the four rooms on the main floor are framed by mantels of golden heart-pine. A narrow, steep stairway leads upstairs to two sleeping rooms.

Theophile Roche, a French weaver who managed the woolen mills, made his home there and used it for his office. During The War Between The States, as Union troops advanced on Roswell on July 6, 1864, Roche hoisted a French flag in an effort to save the mills and his home. Union troops commanded by General Kenner Garrard, under orders from General William Tecumseh Sherman, destroyed the mills but left the house untouched. General Sherman gave his approval for the troops to "hang the wretch (Roche)" if they so desired. His life was spared, but he was arrested for treason and sent north for the duration of the War.

When the war ended, Roche filed a claim for $70,000 in damages with the French and American Claims Commission which he was never able to collect. The mills were rebuilt, the name changed to The Laurel Mills, and the machinery salvaged from the creek. During World War I the mills again manufactured "Roswell Gray" woolens for uniforms as they did during The War Between The States. The mills have since been dismantled.

Mr. and Mrs. Barnett A. Bell purchased the house and restored it during the 1930's, naming their residence Allenbrook.

PLATE II

BARRINGTON HALL

BARRINGTON HALL

On Marietta Street, Facing Mimosa Boulevard

A white arched gateway opens to a long shaded walk leading to Barrington Hall. Fourteen graceful fluted columns extend across the front and along both sides of the Greek Revival mansion in true temple form. The captain's walk on the roof above overlooks the mills, Vickery Creek, and a distant sweep of the Chattahoochee River.

Barrington Hall, home of Barrington King, son of Roswell King, was built by Willis Ball, a master carpenter and architect brought from Connecticut. It was completed in 1842 from timbers cut on the property and aged for two years, the actual construction requiring an additional three years.

Francis Minhinnett, an English landscape gardener and stone mason, laid out the gardens and grounds. There was a smoke house, an icehouse, a kitchen, slave quarters, carriage house, barn, pastures, a vegetable garden and an orchard.

Barrington King moved his wife and family to Roswell from the Georgia coast in 1838. The three-hundred-mile trip was a difficult journey with their nine children, a tutor, the servants, livestock, and household possessions. On their arrival in Roswell, they stayed in Roswell King's log cabin, later called "The Castle" because of the rooms added to accommodate new families as they came.

The Barrington King family afterward moved into a frame cottage built on their property, later used as the kitchen for Barrington Hall. Eight sons and a daughter, Catherine Evelyn, grew to maturity in the large comfortable home, Barrington Hall. During The War Between The States, Mr. and Mrs. King refugeed to the home of their eldest son, the Reverend Charles Barrington King, minister of the White Bluff Presbyterian Church, near Savannah. Of the six King sons serving in the Confederate Army, two were killed in action and two were wounded.

In June, 1865, after a year's absence, Mr. and Mrs. King returned to Roswell thankful their home had been spared by the Union soldiers who had burned the factories. Barrington King set to work at once to rebuild the factory and salvage what he could from their loss. Barrington Hall has come down through the years as the home of descendants of Barrington and Catherine M. King. It is now owned by Miss Katharine Baker Simpson, the great-granddaughter of Barrington King.

PLATE III

BULLOCH HALL

BULLOCH HALL

Bulloch Avenue

Bulloch Hall, built in 1840 by Major James Stephens Bulloch, is recognized as a home of exceptional beauty and heritage. It is one of the few examples in Georgia of the true temple form of architecture with full pedimented portico. The impressive Greek Revival home has four towering Doric columns with pilasters on an immense front piazza.

Major Bulloch, grandson of Georgia Revolutionary Governor Archibald Bulloch, brought his wife Martha and their accumulated children to Roswell from Savannah in 1839. Each had children by a previous marriage and by their marriage there were three children.

The imposing white clapboard home of heart-pine is believed to have been designed by architect Willis Ball. The functional room arrangement was the basic floor plan for most of the homes built in Roswell at that time. A wide central hall is flanked by two large square rooms on each side and two small rooms at the rear, with four bedrooms and a front sewing room upstairs. The lofty center hall with its columned archway often served as a summer living room cooled by the cross ventilation. The home was located upon the highest point in Roswell to take advantage of the river breezes and the lovely view of the foothills.

Major Bulloch did not live to see the marriage of his daughter, Mittie, to Theodore Roosevelt, youngest son of affluent importer Cornelius Van Schaack Roosevelt of New York City. The young couple met through Mittie's half-sister, Susan Elliott, wife of Dr. Hilburn West of Philadelphia, who was related to the Roosevelt family by marriage. The wedding of Mittie and Theodore on December 22, 1853, in the dining room of Bulloch Hall, was the outstanding social event in Roswell's history.

They were the parents of "Teddy" Roosevelt, who would become the twenty-sixth President of the United States. Another son, Elliott Roosevelt, was the father of Anna Eleanor, who married Franklin Delano Roosevelt, the thirty-second President of the United States. President Theodore Roosevelt visited Roswell in 1905 and toured Bulloch Hall, and Mrs. Franklin Delano Roosevelt visited the home on several occasions.

Bulloch Hall was purchased in 1971 by Richard S. Myrick of Atlanta, after being unoccupied for almost twenty years. It was restored and furnished in period pieces, and was opened as a house museum in July, 1972.

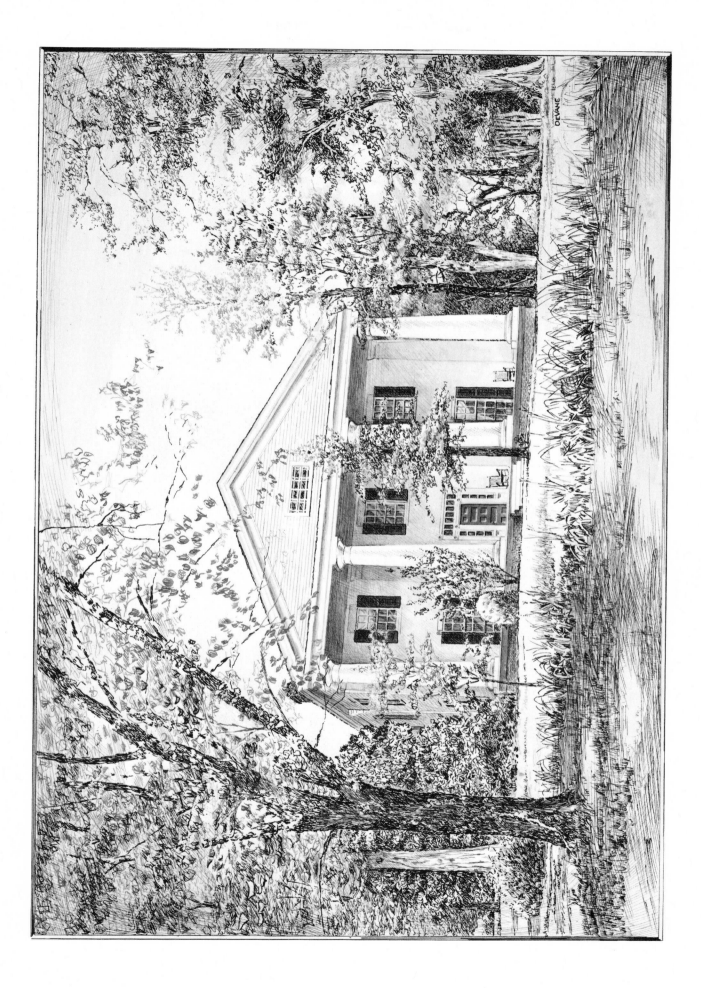

PLATE IV

FOUNDERS' CEMETERY

FOUNDERS' CEMETERY

Sloan Street

The Old Cemetery, or Founders' Cemetery, rests on an oak-shaded knoll above Vickery Creek near the cotton mill. Only the low murmur of the waterfall and the hum of the mill break the stillness of this place where ancient gravestones commemorate some of the first families of Roswell. Their epitaphs tell the stories of these courageous pioneers who buried their loved ones in this new land.

Roswell King, the town's founder, wished to be buried here, and on his tall obelisk monument are these words: "He was the founder of the village which bears his name. A man of great energy, industry and perseverance, of rigid integrity, truth and justice, he early earned and long enjoyed the esteem and confidence of his fellow men."

An outbreak of scarlet fever struck the children of the village in July, 1841, resulting in many deaths. The first death in the colony was that of Charles Irving Bulloch, infant son of Major and Mrs. James Stephens Bulloch, in July, 1841. The Barrington Kings' children, eleven-year-old Nephew and nine-year-old Susan, died the same month. Their graves later were moved from Founders' Cemetery to the new Presbyterian Cemetery behind the church. Dr. and Mrs. Nathaniel Pratt's infant daughter, Catherine, who also died that month, was the first to be buried in the new cemetery. Three-year-old Ralph King Hand, son of Mrs. Eliza Hand, died the following November, and was buried in Founders' Cemetery.

Mrs. James Stephens Bulloch lost her daughter, Georgia Elliott, in September, 1848, and her husband, Major Bulloch, six months later. They were buried near the small grave of Charles Irving Bulloch.

The stone above the graves of John and Jane Dunwody bears the words, "Separated by her death on the 30th of June, 1856, they were reunited to part no more on the 6th of June, 1858."

There are more than twenty graves in the cemetery, many being unmarked graves of family servants. The last recorded burial was that of James A. Burney, only son of Dr. P. J. Burney, marked October 13, 1850 - May 18, 1860.

DE VANE

PLATE V

GOULDING HOUSE

GOULDING HOUSE

Goulding Place

Dr. Francis R. Goulding, minister, author, inventor, sought in Goulding House, or Colonial Place, a final retreat from his demanding life. When he came to Roswell in 1867, he chose for his homesite a wooded knoll a mile from the Presbyterian Church. The property was shaded by the towering trees he loved, and enhanced by a view of the hazy foothills in the distance. In this serene setting he penned his last adventure books and stories of nature, memoirs of boyhood days on the Georgia coast, tales that delighted the children of the world.

His most famous book, "Young Marooners," a juvenile classic translated into foreign languages, was written from 1847 to 1850 during his pastorate at Bath, near Augusta, Georgia. While living in Roswell he wrote "Marooners' Island" in 1868, "Frank Gordon" in 1869, and "The Woodruff Stories" in 1870.

He was born in Sunbury near Midway in 1810, the son of the Reverend Thomas Goulding who taught at the excellent Sunbury Academy and later at Columbia (S.C.) Theological Seminary. Francis Goulding was graduated from Franklin College at Athens and completed his work at Columbia Seminary in 1833, marrying Mary Wallace of Savannah that same year.

In 1842, he invented a sewing machine to lighten the never-ending chores of his wife in caring for their six small children. He neglected having the machine patented, however, and Elias Howe invented and patented a similar machine three years later.

Dr. Goulding became pastor of the Presbyterian Church in Darien after the death of his beloved wife, Mary. He later married Matilda Rees, and during the War lost his home and splendid library when Federal troops burned Darien. While serving as a chaplain to Confederate soldiers in Macon his health failed, and at war's end he retired to Roswell. Though tired, frail, and plagued by asthma, his vast knowledge, his appealing way with children, and his delightful personality never diminished. He spent his last years with his wife and twin daughters at his treasured home, Colonial Place, where he died on August 22, 1881, and was buried in the Roswell Presbyterian Cemetery.

Goulding House, or Colonial Place, is now owned by Mrs. James I. Wright.

PLATE VI

GREAT OAKS

GREAT OAKS

Mimosa Boulevard

The lovely Georgian Colonial home, Great Oaks, built in 1842 by the Reverend and Mrs. Nathaniel Alpheus Pratt, perhaps has played the most versatile role of all. It was originally planned to be another classic columned mansion, but shortly before construction was started the special timbers selected for the home were destroyed by fire. Local clay was tested and found suitable for brick, which were hand-moulded for Great Oaks by slave labor and laid in a unique Flemish bond.

The handsome three-story mansion with front pediment and matching side verandahs has eighteen-inch solid brick walls and heart-pine flooring, panelled doors, and four-inch sills. The carving of the mantels and woodwork is indicative of the skill of the carpenters.

An unusual feature is the "good morning" stairway, where greetings are exchanged at the central landing between the front and back bedroom stairs. The main stairs lead to the landing from the front entrance hall, and a small stairway goes to a side entrance hall. The third floor of the home was used as a three-room dormitory for the seven Pratt sons. Identical front parlors open to the central front hall, and to the rear are study, dining room, and spacious winter kitchen. The outside summer kitchen and outbuildings were connected to the main house by a covered walkway.

Great Oaks is located across the street from the Presbyterian Church, where Dr. Pratt ministered for thirty-nine years. A study and dormitory were constructed on the Pratt property in 1841 near the cottage in which the family lived prior to the completion of Great Oaks. Here Dr. Pratt tutored the sons of friends and relatives from over the state, preparing the young men for Harvard and Princeton.

Though considered a town house, Great Oaks was a sizeable plantation with fields of corn, wheat, and sorghum, and field and house slaves living on the property.

The Pratts remained in their home during The War, even though General Kenner Garrard headquartered there and his troops encamped on the broad shaded lawns.

Ownership of Great Oaks has remained in the Pratt family. Present owners are Mr. Emmett Rushin and his wife, who is the great-granddaughter of the Pratts and great-great-granddaughter of Roswell King.

PLATE VII

HOLLY HILL

HOLLY HILL

Mimosa Boulevard

Holly Hill was built in the 1840's as a summer home for Robert Adams Lewis, a prominent cotton broker of Savannah, who at various times served as acting mayor of that city and as justice of the Inferior Court. His wife, Catherine Barrington Cook, was the niece of Roswell King and the namesake of Mrs. King.

When the Lewises were visiting relatives and old friends in Roswell, they made arrangements with Barrington King to supervise the construction of a summer home. This home, the charming Holly Hill, was built in the "raised cottage" style so popular and practical on the coast. Broad steps lead to the main floor, and on the ground level were originally located the kitchen, dining hall, and larders. A Doric-columned piazza graced by Palladian windows extends across the front, with an identical columned piazza across the back.

Double parlors and two bedrooms on the main floor opened to a central hall, from which extends a curved staircase with slender turned spindles and delicate carved trim. Exquisite architraves of oak leaf and acorn design above the windows and doors prove the superior craftsmanship in the construction of Holly Hill. Mantels of black Italian marble were shipped to Savannah, up the Savannah River to Augusta, and from there to Roswell by oxcart, requiring the labor of many hands before they were placed in the parlors of Holly Hill.

The Lewises were delighted with their home, with the mild, healthful climate of North Georgia, and with the hospitality of the colonists. They decided to live in Roswell permanently, but were forced to leave in 1855 as The War Between The States grew imminent. Georgia friends were interested in the accounts of the marriage of their daughter, Elizabeth Catherine Lewis, to James Audley Maxwell King, grandson of Roswell King, in 1860 at the Lewis mansion on Staten Island, New York. Robert Adams Lewis and his wife spent their last years at the King family home on Colonel's Island, Liberty County, Georgia.

Holly Hill was sold to James Roswell King, son of Barrington King, following the War. The home was restored to its original beauty by the present owner, Mrs. Evelyn Sommerville, and her husband, the late Robert L. Sommerville.

DeVane

PLATE VIII

MIMOSA HALL

MIMOSA HALL

Bulloch Avenue

An aura of serene dignity surrounds Mimosa Hall, reflecting the love and talents of a succession of versatile and affluent owners. Originally named Dunwody Hall by its builder, John Dunwody, the clapboard home burned soon after completion in the early 1840's, and was promptly rebuilt.

The estate adjoins Bulloch Hall, built by Major James Bulloch, Mrs. Dunwody's brother. Willis Ball, an architect from Connecticut who designed Barrington Hall and the Presbyterian Church, is believed to have drawn the plans for Mimosa Hall and Bulloch Hall. He devised functional and convenient floorplans in the classic Greek Revival homes. Large walk-in closets were provided, as well as second stairs from the back halls to the landing of the front stairs, which afforded private passage upstairs for the servants. The basement kitchen in Mimosa Hall still contains the original 1840 iron cooking ware.

The Dunwody home was rebuilt of brick covered with stucco and scored to resemble stone. It was renamed Phoenix Hall for the mythical bird that arose again from the ashes. During The War Between The States, Federal officers were billeted in the home while occupying Roswell.

The house was sold in April, 1869, to General Andrew Jackson Hansell of Marietta, great-great-grandfather of the present owner, and president of the reactivated Roswell Mills. General Hansell, named for General Andrew Jackson, close personal friend of his father, was Adjutant General of Georgia during The War Between The States and served as Representative and State Senator from Cobb County. Mrs. Hansell renamed the home Mimosa Hall for the profusion of mimosa trees in the gardens.

In 1899 the home was sold to Mrs. Ada Prather King, widow of Barrington James King who was Roswell King's grandson. In 1918 the estate was purchased by noted Atlanta architect Neel Reid, who lived there with his mother, Mrs. John Reid. Under Mr. Reid's able direction the wall between the double parlors was removed, creating a spacious forty-foot drawing room with twin fireplaces. Mr. Reid designed the gardens and laid the stone courtyard in the shape of a champagne glass.

Mimosa Hall was acquired in 1947 by Mr. and Mrs. Granger Hansell, whose son and daughter-in-law, Mr. and Mrs. C. Edward Hansell, are the present owners.

PLATE IX

MINTON HOUSE

MINTON HOUSE

Norcross Street

Twenty-year-old John Minton received the sword and the epaulettes of a major in the United States Army in 1817 from the hands of General Andrew Jackson. He had fought gallantly in quelling marauding Creek Indians on the Georgia frontier with General Jackson and the famous Indian fighter, Davy Crockett.

When John Minton was fifteen he saw the militia of Liberty County formed to defend Georgia's coast against British landings in the War of 1812. Living in Sunbury at that time, he perhaps joined the Sunbury Academy students' company. The lad was charged for life with the excitement of combat. During the next fifty years he served in five wars. He was, in 1835, the only man in Liberty County to volunteer aid to Texas in their struggles with Mexico.

Major Minton brought his wife, Rosina Fabian Minton, and children to Roswell in 1849, intending to spend the remainder of his years in farming. He built a comfortable brick cottage with kitchen and slave quarters in the back. A dainty hand-scalloped trim decorated the dormers and cornices. Each of his four children had an upstairs bedroom with a dormer window and a fireplace.

At the outset of The War Between The States, however, John Minton once more offered his services, enlisting as a private in the Confederate Army, as did his three sons. During the first battle at Manassas, Virginia, in July, 1861, he was injured and was sent home. His youngest son, Axson, was killed in the war.

John Minton died on March 5, 1871, and was buried in the Presbyterian Cemetery. His pastor, the Reverend Nathaniel Pratt, said during the services, "Through these wars, especially the last, John Minton was one of the few who came out a better man than he went in."

His oldest friend, Dr. Francis Goulding, in a memorial to him in the *Savannah Daily Republican* on March 29, 1871, penned these words, "The most unselfish person I've ever met was the unqualified verdict of those who knew him best. For he never seemed so happy as when sharing his good things with others."

Minton House is now owned by Mrs. Dennis Lackey.

PLATE X

THE OLD BRICKS

THE OLD BRICKS

Sloan Street

The Bricks, built in 1840 for employees of the Roswell Mills, are among the oldest apartments in the South. The two buildings contain ten apartments, each unit consisting of a kitchen-living room on the first floor and a steep, narrow stairway leading to an upstairs bedroom. Above each of the two fireplaces of handmade brick are thick slab mantels of golden heart-pine. Wide hand-planed pine floors, now burnished by time to a deep luster, still hold the original square nails. The Bricks overlook Vickery Creek and the mill village with its tiny "sharp-top" cottages and narrow winding roads.

During The War, most of the men in the mill village went to join the Confederate Army leaving the mill work in the hands of their wives and children. When Union troops arrived in Roswell, they burned the mills, took over The Bricks for a hospital, and ravaged the mill village. Four hundred mill workers, mostly women and children, were arrested and charged with treason, as the mills were manufacturing materials of war. The moaning, crying workers were loaded into one hundred and ten wagons and hauled to Marietta under guard. There they were given nine days' rations and shipped on troop cars to Indiana where they were released to fend for themselves. Some of them found their way back to Roswell though most were never heard of again.

After the war The Bricks were found to be undamaged, the mill houses reparable. With slight updating of facilities through the years, The Bricks have been in continuous use since 1840.

PLATE XI
PRESBYTERIAN CHURCH

PRESBYTERIAN CHURCH

Mimosa Boulevard

The staunch simplicity of the Doric-columned Presbyterian Church mirrors the faith and dedication of the early Roswell founders. Towering fluted columns and a wide pedimented portico evince the influence of Connecticut architect Willis Ball, who spent several years in Roswell designing Greek Revival mansions for the affluent colonists.

Completed in 1840, the substantial white clapboard sanctuary with its short, square bell-tower resembles the early New England meeting houses. Hand-carved woodwork and solid panelled doors bear witness to the expert craftsmen of the day. The high center pulpit, the box pews, and the gallery for slave members are strikingly similar to those of the Midway Congregational Church linked so closely to Roswell's heritage.

A ship's bell cast in bronze in 1827 by John Wilbank of Philadelphia, Pennsylvania, was presented to the Roswell Church by the Independent Presbyterian Church of Savannah. Its mellow tones called Sunday worshippers and summoned carriage drivers to the front portico after the services and it tolled in slow cadence for each funeral cortege. The bell still is rung on Sundays.

The early Roswell Presbyterians invited Dr. Nathaniel Alpheus Pratt, pastor of the Darien Presbyterian Church, to become their pastor. The Reverend Pratt, with his wife, the former Catherine Barrington King, daughter of Roswell King, visited Roswell in October, 1839, and met with fifteen colonists in the parlor of Primrose Cottage to organize the Presbyterian Church. The church and The Academy, Roswell's first school, were built on land donated for this purpose by Roswell King and his son, Barrington King. The Reverend A. H. Hand of Augusta was the first teacher in the two-room schoolhouse.

Dr. Pratt preached his first sermon in the newly completed sanctuary on May 17, 1840, his last sermon there thirty-nine years later, a short time before his death on August 30, 1879.

During the War, Union troops used the church for a hospital, removing the pews and destroying the organ and the hymnals. Fortunately, a church member, Miss Fannie Whitmire, had hidden the communion silver which had been given to the church in 1840 by friends. Convalescing soldiers painted a checkerboard on the door of a Sunday School cupboard, the outline of it still visible today.

The original sanctuary continues to serve the congregation of the Roswell Presbyterian Church. The Reverend Cyrus S. Mallard, Jr., is the present minister.

DeVane

PLATE XII

PRIMROSE COTTAGE

PRIMROSE COTTAGE

Mimosa Boulevard

Primrose Cottage, the first permanent home built in Roswell, was completed in seven months for the widowed Mrs. Eliza King Hand, daughter of Roswell King. Laborers were brought from other jobs during the winter of 1839 in order to hasten the construction of the home for Mrs. Hand, whose husband, Bayard Hand, had died recently in Darien. Mrs. Hand, her three small children, and her father moved into the home in August.

The simple and comfortable New England-style house was the type familiar to Roswell King during his early years in Connecticut. Four large, square rooms downstairs and four upstairs opened to wide central halls. Early colonists organized the Roswell Presbyterian Church here in the parlor of Primrose Cottage in October, 1839.

Peter Minhinnett, a carpenter, and his brother, Francis, a landscape gardener and stonemason, came from Plymouth, England, to help build the homes and gardens. One of the things Peter Minhinnett constructed was an exquisite hand-turned bannister fence of Rosemary pine across the front of the Primrose Cottage property. His wife disliked the pioneering life in Roswell, however, and they soon returned to England.

A wide, oak-shaded verandah extends across the back of the home, a favorite gathering place for family and friends through the years. Roswell King enjoyed the leisure hours spent here during his last years. He died on February 15, 1844, at seventy-eight years of age and was buried in Founders' Cemetery.

Dr. Charles T. Quintard, an affluent young man from Connecticut, stayed with the Hands at Primrose Cottage while working with Dr. William King, son of Barrington King. He eventually was married to Eliza Catherine, Mrs. Hand's daughter. Dr. Quintard later became an Episcopal minister, a chaplain during The War, and Bishop of Tennessee and Vice Chancellor of The University of the South at Sewanee, Tennessee. The widowed Mrs. Hand married Nicholas J. Bayard of Savannah and they remained at Primrose Cottage until The War.

It is now owned and occupied by the Charles King family.

PLATE XIII

ROSWELL STORES

ROSWELL STORES

Atlanta Street

The original Roswell store, a commissary for the mill workers, shows the builders' diligent attention to detail. The simple two-story brick building, constructed in 1839, takes on a classic appearance with its delicate square pilasters and dentil design at the cornices. The store overlooks the town square, and originally a shaded area at the side of the store provided a space for shoppers' horses and rigs. A shed roof with braced posts extends over the sidewalk made of massive creek stones.

A selection of luxury items as well as staples were offered as the other buildings were added. A gentleman could outfit himself with a linen or alpaca coat, an embroidered vest, a fine hat of beaver, panama, or moleskin. He could buy tobacco, pistols, rifles, caps and gunpowder, as well as implements and tools.

Lady shoppers could find French calico, gloves, embroidered berthas and shawls, bonnets and ribbons. They could buy Swiss muslins, colognes, balms, combs and brushes. The children spent their coins on gumdrops and taffy and on the exciting new drink called soda water.

Liniments, ointments, and medicines were sold, as well as housewares such as coffee mills, knives and forks, oil lamps and wax matches. The stores offered a limited line of caskets for the deceased and a selection of tasteful mourning wear for the bereaved.

The last of the three buildings, a large two-story structure with outside stairway and with iron pilasters across the front, was added in the early 1900's. Part of the first floor served as the post office, the remainder a drugstore-soda shop.

The original post office for the area was located at nearby Lebanon, and in 1847 was moved to Roswell. Mail was delivered to the post office from the Marietta railroad station three times a week by a two-horse hack line, a conveyance shared by travelers coming to Roswell.

The Roswell Stores were purchased by Historic Roswell, Inc., in 1972, were restored and opened as specialty shops.

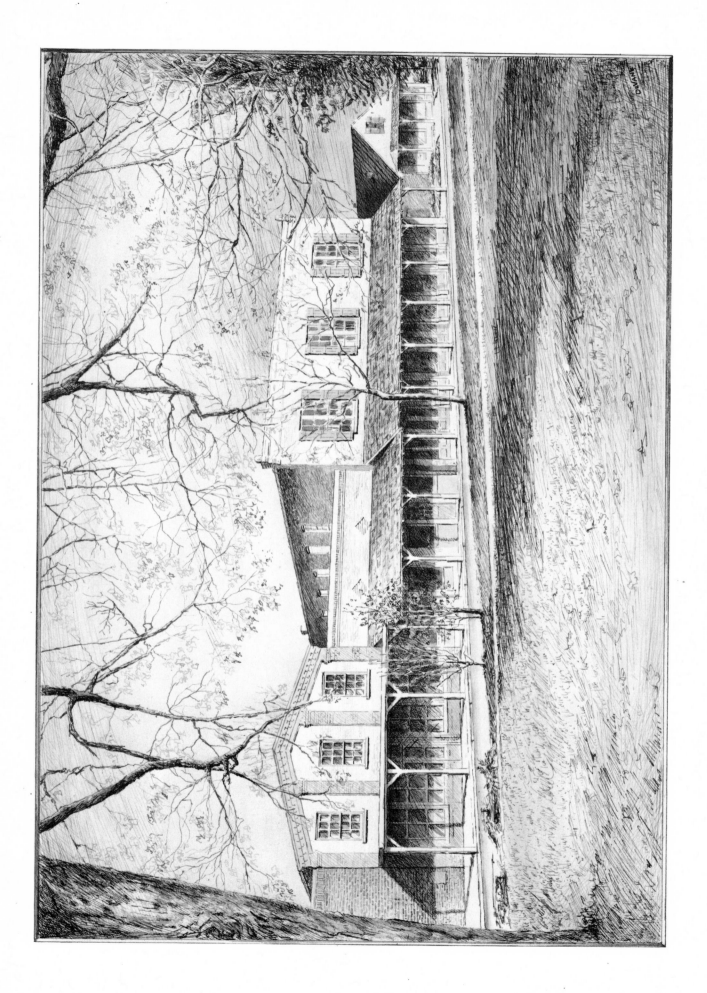

PLATE XIV

WATERFALL AND MILL RUINS

WATERFALL AND MILL RUINS

Vickery Creek

A thirty-foot dam and waterfall with a wooden millrace was constructed on Vickery Creek in the summer of 1835 to supply power for the Roswell cotton mills which were completed three years later. Construction of the earth-and-rock-filled dam was a feat of engineering and architectural skill, accomplished in a wilderness still inhabited by Cherokee Indians.

Roswell King supervised the meager group of workers as they toiled with bare hands and simple tools. Upstream they built temporary cofferdams of rock-filled logs to divert the creek into a sluice. At the dam-site massive timbers were stacked across the creekbed, and layer upon layer of earth, rocks, and debris were heaped behind the barricade, forming a solid, water-tight mass. Boulders and stones of varying sizes were stacked and wedged into an impregnable wall thirty feet high in front of the wood- and earth-filled barricade.

The released water rushed over the dam forming the waterfall. A gate diverted water from the dam into the millrace and on to the mill below, turning the giant waterwheel which drove the spindles and looms. By 1850, the Roswell Mills, one of twenty cotton mills in Georgia, was devouring five bales of cotton a day and turning out thousands of yards of shirting, osnaburgs, and yarn. It employed one hundred and fifty workers who labored eleven hours a day manufacturing superior goods sent to Tennessee, Alabama, and to various parts of Georgia.

The sounds of the mill could be heard throughout the village, as a warning bell signaled the starting of the roaring, humming, drumming machinery. Occasionally the creek waters ran low, the waterwheel stopped turning, and the mill was shut down. At other times, flash floods in the hills would send water thundering down the creek and gushing through the millrace with tremendous force. During one such day, on August 18, 1862, an English lad, twenty-four-year-old John Henry Lang, a mill employee, fell into the millrace and was drowned. He was buried in the King family plot at the Presbyterian Cemetery.

The Roswell Mills were burned by Union troops on July 6, 1864, and only one original structure remains. The mill, rebuilt ten years later, was struck by lightning and burned again in 1926. The Southern Mills, built nearby in 1882, still is in operation.